PONY UP

Mallory Jane Weiss

D1491250

BROADWAY PLAY PUBLISHING INC
New York
www.broadwayplaypublishing.com
info@broadwayplaypublishing.com

PONY UP
© Copyright 2023 Mallory Jane Weiss

First edition: December 2023
I S B N: 979-8-88856-003-7

Book design: Marie Donovan
Page make-up: Adobe InDesign
Typeface: Palatino

PONY UP was first produced in 2019 at the School of Drama, The New School. The cast and creative contributors were:

RUTHIE...Katharine Chin
PEARL.. Tori Ernst
ROOSTER...Hallie Schwartz
JACK...Ryan Nicholas Cooper
TROUT.. Christopher F Costa
ACE .... Collin McConnell
COW/CALF... Hyojin Park

Director... Andrés López-Alicea
Scenic design..Raphael Mishler
Costume design... Grier Coleman
Lighting design ....Dante Olivia Smith
Sound design..Megan Culley
Assistant Director...................Francisco Rivera Rodriguez
Stage Manager .... Jonathan Castanien
Mentor ....Sarah Gancher

ACKNOWLEDGEMENTS

Meohmymeohmy…I'm one lucky gal to have so many silly and supportive people in my corner. And this play would not exist without y'all.

First and foremost, thank you to my parents—Barb and Marc—for believing in me and my big dreams. I appreciate every time you both put me on a horse. (Metaphorically, that is. The literal horseback riding I could've lived without.) To Jack and Jay, thank you for laughing with and at me; you're the best brothers around.

Thank you to Alice Stites and Lizzy Weingold for having vision in spades. I am so fortunate to be on a (nameless) team with two smart, savvy, sensitive women.

This play would not exist if not for the support and resources I received at The New School for Drama. Thank you to the mentors, designers, crew, administrative staff, and artists that helped bring this piece to life.

My heartfelt thanks to the original cast—Katharine, Tori, Hallie, Ryan, Chris, Collin, and Hyojin—for caring about these characters and for making this play funnier and deeper at every turn. To the play's first director, Andrés, you helped create a beautiful and magical world; this play grew thanks to your keen eye, kind heart, and unmatched rhythm.

To Collin, Miles, and Conlan...I am grateful every day to have spent three years with you three. Thank you for your notes and the beers, for reading my women with grace, and for guiding me in general. Y'all are the worst/best.

A special thanks to Coops, my largest fan. Thank you for the title, the goofiest times, and for encouraging me to get an ice cream sandwich instead of giving up on this play. I am so lucky to call you *partner*. (Western theme, get it?)

And to my friends—oh, my friends—this is a play for and because of you. Thank you for the schemes, the heists, and the hijinks. Thank you for holding me through heartbreak, for finding different plans for the same dream, for celebrating with me when we land at the coast. I love our friendship most of all. Yeehaw.

CHARACTERS

RUTHIE HOLLIDAY, *woman, 20s; sharp; self-conscious; unaware of her natural talents; like the spark of the fire; (wife to* JACK OWENS*)*

PEARL HART, *woman, mid to late 20s; hungry; feisty but not rough; like the dancing part of the flame*

ROOSTER PARKHURST, *woman, late 20s/early 30s; fierce; loyal; like the blue part of the flame; (sister to* TROUT PARKHURST*)*

COW, *woman, can be played by an actor between the ages of 20 and 100; curious; wise; like the embers in the charcoal*

JACK OWENS, *man, 20s/30s; competitive; entitled; like the match—can be snapped in two as easily as it can be struck; (husband to* RUTHIE HOLLIDAY*)*

TROUT PARKHURST, *man, late 20s/early 30s; lost but not boyish; stubborn; like the smoldering log; (brother to* ROOSTER PARKHURST*)*

ACE FISHER, *man, 20s/30s; ludicrous; harmless; like the tinder that pops and hisses*

CALF, *woman; innocent; eager; like the twigs aflame. Played by the actor who plays* COW*.*

SETTING

(The wild) west of somewhere.

Simultaneously the 1880s and the future.

A wild west. Hot, dry, arid. It's all yellow, orange, and red. Even the cacti are hot. And there should be cacti, perhaps made of cardboard, perhaps punctured with Christmas lights. Dust, tumbleweeds. The whole thing should crunch. It should look thirsty. Allow for whimsy; allow for kitsch.

Music should be Americana and country and folk. Strings and gruff voices.

Train tracks aren't restricted to being flat or straight. It can be a rollercoaster. It can be barbed wire. Bicycles can be hung on the walls.

But the whole wild west should feel constricted, locked-in on all sides. Any world outside is a fantasy, is the dream, is the mission.

&

the coast.

A coast. Farther west. The ocean, a cool breeze. Blues, greens, purples. Clouds, maybe even the threat of a rain shower. Sand, seashells, fish, algae, etc.

The music has an echo. There's room inside of it.

Give the imagination room. A make-believe ocean will quench our thirst far more readily.

NOTES

"I was only twenty-two years old. I was good-looking, desperate, discouraged, and ready for anything that might come. I do not care to dwell on this period of my life. It is sufficient to say that I went from one city to another until some time later I arrived in Phoenix."
—Pearl Hart

"The article noted how unusual it was that Parkhurst could have lived so long with no one discovering his assigned sex, and to "achieve distinction in an occupation above all professions calling for the best physical qualities of nerve, courage, coolness and endurance, and that she should add to them the almost romantic personal bravery that enables one to fight one's way through the ambush of an enemy..." was seen to be almost beyond believing, but there was ample evidence to prove the case."
—Wikipedia, on the discovery that Charley Parkhurst was a woman

"...We live in a world in which there is a good deal for women to object to, including the fact that a lot of men wish to harm and humiliate and subjugate us, but responding to that comes with its own penalties. When a woman shows anger, Chemaly observes, "she automatically violates gender norms. She is met with

aversion, perceived as more hostile, irritable, less competent, and unlikable." But even if, for example, she says quite calmly that gender violence is epidemic, she can still be attacked and characterized as angry, and that anger can be used as a way to discount the evidence, in a society that often still expects that women be pleasing and compliant...."
—Rebecca Solnit, "All the Rage", *The New Yorker*

"Most great activists—from Ida B Wells to Dolores Huerta to Harvey Milk to Bill McKibben—are motivated by love, first of all. If they are angry, they are angry at what harms the people and phenomena they love, but their urges are primarily protective, not vengeful. Love is essential; anger is perhaps optional."
—Rebecca Solnit, "All the Rage", *The New Yorker*

one.
a train headed west

(*A train whistle. The rhythm of the train moving along the tracks.*)

(*The smoker car. Everything is obscured by smoke.*)

(JACK *is surrounded by the shadows of other men. Silhouettes*)

(RUTHIE *is the only woman. And she feels it.*)

(*The men play billiards.* JACK *hits a winning shot. He holds out his hand to accept his winnings.*)

JACK:
Pony up.
Should've known better than to challenge me today, gentlemen.
I cannot lose today.

(JACK *turns to* RUTHIE *and plants a big, wet kiss on her cheek.*)

RUTHIE: (*Bashful*)
Jack

JACK:
Ain't she cute? Ain't I a lucky son-of-a-gun?
Tell the fellas, Ruthie. Tell 'em how
pool is about confidence and natural talent
general know-how

and the ability to
handle a shaft of a
certain size

RUTHIE:

Someone's in a good mood.

JACK:

Damn straight, I'm in a good mood.

(JACK *hands* RUTHIE *his pool cue.*)

RUTHIE:

game's over, right?
can we—?

JACK:

almost, almost.
like I was saying
everyone was sittin' on hot coals. Just waitin' for the
trio, right?

RUTHIE:

three of the biggest horses we'd ever seen
like nothing we'd—

JACK:

don't interrupt don't interrupt
these things have a flow to them
I'm building suspense.

RUTHIE:

sorry sorry
keep going

JACK:

Biggest horses this world's ever seen. Almost
unnatural how big.
Felt like discovering a new land. I'm an explorer. A
conqueror.

(RUTHIE *lines up a shot with* JACK's *cue. She hits it. She
looks up, pleased.*)

RUTHIE:
Neither of us can lose today.

JACK:
You got chalk on the table, honey.

RUTHIE:

oh, sorry.
out of practice.

(RUTHIE *licks her thumb to wipe off the table.* JACK *stops her.*)

JACK:
shouldn't be "practicing" at all, right fellas?
you fellas hear about the girl up north?
saddled up her pop's horse while the man was
sleeping on the porch
barely got a hundred yards away before he had her
tied to the tracks.
now, it's always a shame when it's a family matter
but the law's the law, right, fellas?

RUTHIE:

but you would never

JACK:

now I ain't saying it's—
women ride bicycles.
men ride horses.
the way of the world.

(RUTHIE *takes one of* JACK's *hands.*)

RUTHIE:
but these, gentle hands?

(JACK *takes his hand from* RUTHIE *and grabs the pool cue from her.*)

JACK:
So like I was saying—

had to rebuild the stables in the barn
just to fit their massive, massive—

RUTHIE:

and three different colors
speckled grey one is going to be Cyclone—we named
them after weather because—

JACK:

Now had they told me they were gonna take my
picture
well, I would've worn a different tie.
You see this one here's so shiny, it just done bounced
the flash right off it.
Pop pop pop
cameras in every direction.
The photo still came out okay, of course…at least, the
Herald must've thought so
puttin' it on the cover and all.
Bumped that story about the girl up north to below-
the-fold.

RUTHIE:

Did you show them? Have they seen it?
He looked just like…

(RUTHIE *grabs* JACK's *cigarette and imitates what* JACK
*looks like on the cover of the paper. She takes a drag on the
cigarette.* JACK *snatches it away from her.*)

JACK:

(*A performance for the fellas*)
real men always have the reins in one hand
and a cigarette in the other.

RUTHIE:

not as tall as you, but that's pretty much exactly what
you—

JACK:

You'll have to excuse Ruthie, gentleman.

Been a lot of excitement.
She ain't herself.
You want to go back to the compartment, honey?

RUTHIE:
thought you said you weren't done

JACK:
Let me walk her back to our compartment, fellas.
Give me a chance to grab the copy of the *Herald*
see if that picture really is better than the one in the
Daily Tribune.

(JACK *and* RUTHIE *exit the train compartment, into a
narrow hallway.*)

JACK:
knew you should've stayed in the compartment
you can't go/smoking a man's

RUTHIE:
like one of your horses in her stable?

JACK:
you ain't one of my horses—you're my wife.

RUTHIE:
it was a joke, Jack
I was just playing. I'm sorry.

JACK:
These are important men.
You see how they're looking up to me?
That's how big I am.

RUTHIE:
Well, I think they're disgusting
cackling at that girl getting tied to the tracks
scowling at me for one puff
they're foul
and I'm glad you're nothing like them.

JACK:

don't be talking like that

RUTHIE:

since when

JACK:

since I said so.

(*Beat*)

RUTHIE:

I'm going for a walk

JACK:

where

RUTHIE:

up and down the hall

JACK:

never met a more restless woman

RUTHIE:

I'll be less restless when I'm on the back of a stallion

JACK:

that so?

RUTHIE:

something about the wind, the height, and the horizon
I just know it

(*Beat*)

JACK:

gonna get the *Herald* for the fellas

(JACK *kisses the top of* RUTHIE's *head before they part in separate directions.*)

RUTHIE:

still mad at you

JACK:

that so?

RUTHIE:

you didn't pull me into that picture

JACK:

what picture?

RUTHIE:

for the papers.

JACK:

I didn't arrange the photo.
You know that.
I stood up and smiled, that's all.
Because I was happy.
I can't help who takes a picture of me and when.
Is that what you think?
That I didn't pull you into the photo on purpose?

RUTHIE:

I don't know

JACK:

because that'd be crazy.
Look at you. Who wouldn't want a picture of this?

RUTHIE:

I was supposed to be your partner.
That's all. And now it looks like...

JACK:

You are.
Come on, honey. We were celebrating.
Those stallions are gonna be my legacy.
Our legacy.
That's the dream, ain't it? You and me, riding off into
the sunset?
Off somewhere bigger and quiet
where there ain't so much noise.
At least, that's what I thought we were doing.

RUTHIE:

Sorry. You're right.

JACK:

go stretch your legs
don't want to keep the fellas waiting.

RUTHIE:

We'll get a picture when I ride, right? Not for the papers
but for us, right? I bought a hat.

JACK:

Sure. We'll see.

RUTHIE:

We'll see about the picture or…?

JACK:

They're waiting on me, baby doll.

RUTHIE:

Sorry, sorry. Go.

(JACK *makes his way toward his train compartment.* RUTHIE *drifts off in the other direction, head down. Meanwhile….*)

(PEARL, *dressed like a proper rancher's daughter, makes her way through the cramped halls of a train. She carries a large suitcase and wheels a bicycle.*)

(*Men, shadows and silhouettes, line the halls smoking and drinking and taking up space.*)

(PEARL *tries to maneuver through them. She feels as though someone might be following her, might have recognized her. She can't quite glance over her shoulder.*)

(*Men seem to close in around her.*)

(*She spots the train compartment where* JACK *exited. She peeks in, sees it's empty.*)

(PEARL *ducks into it.*)

(*She takes a beat to register that she's safe in the compartment. She takes a deep breath.*)

(*Then, she looks up and sees* JACK'*s jacket (inside one pocket is the bag of money he won in the pool game).*)

(PEARL *smiles. She has an idea. She opens her suitcase and pulls out a bandana. She ties it around her face, like an outlaw. She's all about the spectacle.*)

(PEARL *sneaks toward the jacket. She checks the window to make sure no one is coming. She's safe. She searches the pockets and finds the money. She celebrates.*)

(*As she does so,* JACK *returns, his face buried in the newspaper.*)

(PEARL *quickly pulls the bandana off her face and hides the money behind her back.*)

JACK:
honey, the bastards thought the *Herald* took
four inches off my height
can you—?
(*He looks up at the woman he's talking to.*)
you ain't my wife

PEARL: (*Facetious*)
no, but I could be

JACK:
that so?
tell me—what do you think of this photo?

PEARL:
digging for compliments?

JACK:
heard they're worth more from beautiful women

PEARL:

don't you have a wife?

JACK:

not opposed to an admirer.

(JACK *shows* PEARL *the newspaper. She tries to keep the money hidden. It's too close for comfort.*)

JACK:

what do you think?

PEARL:

well look at you.

JACK:

impressed?

(JACK *gets even closer.* PEARL *shoves the newspaper at him, defensively.*)

PEARL:

"Tallest Man In Town"
put a lot of effort into that?
seems like maybe biology did most of the work for you

(PEARL *sits on top of the money bag, waiting for the moment when she can put it in her suitcase.*)

JACK:

you know you've got
the beauty of a cactus blossom
but the prick of its needles

PEARL:

(Just sarcastic enough)
oh, I'm sorry

(JACK *turns for a moment to put down the paper.* PEARL *quickly opens her suitcase. She doesn't have enough time to put the money in before* JACK *turns back around. She plays it cool.*)

(JACK *stares at* PEARL.)

JACK:

you look mighty familiar

PEARL:

you say that to all the women you meet on the train?

JACK:

but I only mean it with you.

PEARL:

how flattering

JACK:

there are those needles again.
smile, honey; we're just friends here
(Beat)
you could make it up to me—

PEARL:

oh?

JACK:

I'd take a kiss on the cheek from a gal with eyes like
yours

PEARL:

no thank you

JACK:

you're right
kiss on the cheek ain't enough

PEARL:

not what I meant

JACK:

come on
you picked the right compartment

PEARL:

didn't know it was yours

JACK:
then you're luckier than you thought
it was a mighty big auction I won, you know

PEARL:
so I've heard

JACK:
don't you want to ask me
how big?

PEARL:
almost at my stop, actually

JACK:
where you headed?

PEARL:
west

JACK:
whole train's headed west

PEARL:
then I'm on the right train

JACK:
You don't want to take a tone with me.

(PEARL *smirks. Maybe she laughs.*)

JACK:
what?

PEARL:
the way you said that.
you believe it so
completely

(JACK *steps away. He barely turns away before he turns back
to* PEARL.)

JACK:
I swear I know you from somewhere
what did you say your name was?

PEARL:

I didn't

JACK:

I've seen that face before

PEARL:

close your eyes

JACK:

why?

PEARL:

maybe I want to know
what it's like to kiss
the tallest man in town

JACK:

that so?

PEARL:

Isn't that what you wanted?

JACK:

well aren't you full of surprises

(JACK *closes his eyes.* PEARL *makes sure he can't see her.*
She stands. But before she can put the money away, his eyes
burst open.)

JACK:

wait a minute
(He looks down at the money then back at PEARL.*)*
someone's looking for you
Pearl Hart?

(JACK *grabs* PEARL *by the shoulders.)*

PEARL:

let me go

(PEARL *draws a pistol out of nowhere.* JACK *lets her go, but*
remains threatening, as she locks her suitcase.)

JACK:
Your daddy know you took that pistol?
I don't remember exactly how much he put on that
poster
in exchange for his daughter's safe return
to her ivory tower
but judging by that school on your suitcase
I bet it'd buy me a barn made of silver spoons.

(PEARL *slowly makes her way toward the door with her suitcase, still holding the gun at* JACK. *She glances at her bicycle. She has to leave it behind.*)

PEARL:
You think you know who I am?
You think I'm pink all over, my hair's spun gold.
Well, I'm more than all that. Or I'm gonna be.

JACK:
That so?

PEARL:
That's so.
Don't you try and follow me.

(PEARL *exits the train compartment.* PEARL *and* RUTHIE *share a brief glance.* JACK *appears in the doorway.*)

JACK:
honey,
was just wondering where you'd gotten off to

(RUTHIE *enters the train compartment. She sees the bicycle.*)

RUTHIE:
Should you go after her?

JACK:
Who?

RUTHIE:
the woman that left this bicycle.

JACK:

Oh that? She's an admirer
a fan
a woman that read that I'm the man to—
someone who knows I'm important
that I'm handy, that's all.
Brakes squeak. Offered to fix it for her.

RUTHIE:

since when do you fix bicycles?

JACK:

I fix yours, don't I?
I swear—you seem hell-bent on making me the villain
today.
Of all days.

RUTHIE:

sorry

JACK:

you like me, remember?

RUTHIE:

I remember.

JACK:

Hell, sometimes you love me.

RUTHIE:

all times.

JACK:

well okay then.

(*Beat*)

RUTHIE:

A lot of people are reading the *Herald* in the dining car.

JACK:

Yeah?
Good.

RUTHIE:
Made me want to rip the papers out of everyone's
hands
snatch 'em right up

JACK:
Why? Your husband's a celebrity, now.

RUTHIE:
I don't like to share.

JACK:
you've forgiven me, then?
for the picture in the paper?

RUTHIE:
suppose I have.
(Beat)
What did the fellas think of the *Herald*?

JACK:
Said it was fine

RUTHIE:
that's all?

JACK:
Yes

RUTHIE:
Sorry

(Beat)

JACK:
I'm tired of this trip.
Seems like trains should move faster than this.

(RUTHIE *looks out the window.*)

RUTHIE:
we're almost back
you can tell by the way the sun catches on the dust
the way everything burns orange

the way the weeds are singed at the top
like everything's being eaten slowly by heat and time.
it's why the radio crackles with static
why the cacti vibrate with voltage
why it's so damn hot and so damn still.

(*Beat*)

JACK:
you describing Hell or home?

(*Beat*)

RUTHIE:
sorry. guess I'm sick of this trip too,
that's all.

JACK:
next time, we get a private compartment
and a fruit plate
and those cut vegetables with the dipping sauce
or
better
I'll ride alongside the train, race it down the tracks
and you can wave and whistle from the window

RUTHIE:
Jack Owens, your visions get more and more
outrageous by the minute
besides, what would I do in this compartment all by
myself?

JACK:
you're right
I better keep you company.
we'll bring our own locks.
we won't have any interruptions
none of this nonsense with strangers and bicycles.

(JACK *wraps himself around* RUTHIE. *She looks over at the
mysterious bicycle. She strokes his hair absent-mindedly.*)

RUTHIE:
any other visions under your hat?

JACK:
hm?

RUTHIE:
tell me about what you think I'll look like on top of a
horse.

JACK:
later, honey.
been a long trip.
let me close my eyes a bit.

two.
the bicycle shop

(ROOSTER *fills a bicycle tire with a manual pump. Bored.*
Angry.)

(*She pretends the bicycle pump is the plunger-trigger to a*
box of dynamite.)

(*She makes sweeping gestures, pretending to blow up the*
shop.)

(*Just as* ROOSTER *is about to die her martyr death, the bell*
on the door jingles. ROOSTER *turns to see* PEARL *in the*
doorway.)

PEARL:
I'm in need of a bicycle

ROOSTER:
(*Could not be more excited to see her*)
go fuck yourself

(PEARL *and* ROOSTER *run and hug each other.*)

ROOSTER:

took you long enough

PEARL:

left my bicycle on the train

ROOSTER:

why?

(PEARL *reveals the bag of money to* ROOSTER.)

PEARL:

was in a hurry

ROOSTER:

what is this?

PEARL:

your letter said you wanted to stir up trouble.

ROOSTER:

petty theft is not what I meant

PEARL:

well I'm an outlaw now, so
what've you got in black?

ROOSTER:

how about a horse?

PEARL:

very funny.

ROOSTER:

I'm serious

PEARL:

Rooster

ROOSTER:

you read the *Herald*?

PEARL:

met him, actually

ROOSTER:

how?!

PEARL:

I was in his compartment
briefly

ROOSTER:

so the money's his

PEARL:

he left it unattended

ROOSTER:

you sure know how to pick 'em

PEARL:

why do you care?

ROOSTER:

he lives right on the border
right along the train tracks.

PEARL:

so

ROOSTER:

Those horses, his horses, could carry us

PEARL:

where?

ROOSTER:

out

PEARL:

"out"

ROOSTER:

the coast

PEARL:

you want to go to "the coast"

ROOSTER:

don't say it like that

PEARL:
how else are you supposed to talk about a myth?

ROOSTER:
why do you think the most powerful men live on the
border?

PEARL:
the view

ROOSTER:
of the cacti?

PEARL:
sunsets unimpeded
I don't know

ROOSTER:
to keep us in. to keep us here.

PEARL:
Your letter said—
I thought you just
missed me.
I thought you wanted to stir up some trouble
like when we were kids. Hop a fence. Rob a train.
live like

ROOSTER:
outlaws?
I do.
but this isn't a game.
This isn't pretend.

PEARL:
and the law?
you want to get us tied to the tracks?

ROOSTER:
I don't plan on getting caught.
We get out.
For real. Not the edge of town.

Not the desert.
The coast.

PEARL:

If it even exists.

ROOSTER:

It exists.
We ride out of town
as far as we can go.
then it's
nothing but horizon.
(Beat)
unless of course that sounds too...

PEARL:

what?

ROOSTER:

I would understand if that didn't sound
like your cup of tea

PEARL:

and why wouldn't it sound like my
cup of tea?

ROOSTER:

I don't know what that fancy school did to your
natural affinity for
rebellion.
Maybe you're
homesick for your parents' ranch out East

PEARL:

heavens-fuck.
I'm more than silver and lace and acres.
Not only am I an outlaw, but I am an outlaw with an
elite education.
So, storm's coming.

ROOSTER:

yeah?
so then how about those horses?

PEARL:

you don't ever crack, do you?

ROOSTER:

I've been waiting for the right moment, Pearl
waiting for the right horses
the best shot.
and this is it.
now are you in or—?

(TROUT *and* ACE *enter.* ACE, *with a flourish. His mouth is full of a giant carrot that he chomps on with unnecessary vigor.*)

ACE:

(Like a rodeo announcer)
Ladies and gentleman
welcome to the bicycle shop
where we welcome home
the only man who can call himself a champion in
saddle bronc riding
steer wrestling
and tie-down roping
sixteen-time, I repeat, sixteen-time winner of
rodeo's sexiest man of the west
and all-time best friend in my heart
Trout fucking Parkhurst.

(TROUT *and* ACE *exchange some sort of childhood handshake.*)

ACE:

You're home, and I love it.
I've got big plans for us, buddy, big plans.
I cannot believe you're back. Look at you. In the flesh.
Phenomenal flesh. The flesh of a champion.

>   ROOSTER:
get a room.

(ACE *goes up to* ROOSTER. *He chomps down on the carrot in
her face.*)

>   ACE:
and, of course, the remarkable Rooster

>   ROOSTER:
Ace,
you know what they say about men who start to look
like their horses?

>   ACE:
Trout, your sister thinks I'm handsome

>   PEARL:
who is this guy?

>   ROOSTER:
no one.

>   ACE:
and you are?

(ACE *kisses* PEARL's *hand*)

>   TROUT: *(To* ROOSTER*)*
miss me?

>   PEARL:
Pearl./
grew up down the street from these two
back in the day

>   ROOSTER: *(To* TROUT*)*
surprised you actually showed up

>   TROUT: *(To* ACE/PEARL*)*
Before her daddy dug up enough gold to plate the sun.

>   PEARL:
How's the rodeo?

TROUT:

it'll survive without me

PEARL:

you retired?

TROUT:

something like that

PEARL:

serendipitous timing...

TROUT:

where are all the customers?

ROOSTER:

excuse me?

TROUT:

And I remember this place being bigger
Was it bigger?

ROOSTER:

it was before your ego squeezed its way through the
door

TROUT:

you ain't a little happy to see me?

ROOSTER:

oh I'm sorry
I forgot that my job was crowing in the dawn for your
new day
cock-a-fucking-doodle do
welcome home

TROUT:

dunno why you're mad at me

ROOSTER:

well, for one thing
your postcard said you were arriving yesterday.
two "v"s in arriving.

ACE:

easy, easy—
this man's been hit in the head –
a lot. You're lucky it was only two v's.

ROOSTER:

Don't you have somewhere to be?

ACE:

In fact, yes.
we're gonna go lift some heavy shit in the back
work up a musk, you know
pheromones and shit.
Prime our muscles for our meeting at the saloon
tomorrow.
Helps us look taller.

TROUT:

meeting?
you got him to—?

ACE:

would I let you down?

TROUT: (To ROOSTER)

Make sure you're around tomorrow
I got business to—

ROOSTER:

Mr Rodeo Star
You ain't on the circuit. Shop's your problem now.

TROUT:

just 'cause I own this place
ain't mean I'm gonna work here.
I got bigger plans than this. You'll see.

ROOSTER:

World doesn't revolve around your big, stupid head.

TROUT:

"Big, stupid head"…

You know, you could decide to be in a good mood.
That's all it would take.

ROOSTER:

no thank you.

(TROUT *and* ACE *exit to the back room of the store.)*

PEARL:

Trout's commandeered the store.

ROOSTER:

not like I ever really owned it anyway

PEARL:

so now, you—

ROOSTER:

got nothin' keeping me.
ain't got nothin left
except…

PEARL:

except.

ROOSTER:

Except…

(Beat)

PEARL:

Fine…I'm in.

ROOSTER:

in?

PEARL:

the horses. the horizon.
I'm in.

ROOSTER:

yeah?

PEARL:

yeah

(*All of a sudden, music blares from the back room, where* TROUT *and* ACE *are working out. A heavy western rock [think: Zac Brown Band's "Heavy is the Head" or "Junkyard"].* ROOSTER *and* PEARL *endure the music, while scheming with their backs to the bicycle shop's door. They shout to be heard.*)

ROOSTER:

fuck yeah!

PEARL:

what's the plan?!

ROOSTER:

what?!

PEARL:

the plan!

ROOSTER:

poison him! so he sleeps!

PEARL:

how?!

ROOSTER:

not now! When we're ready!

PEARL:

(*Referring to the music*)
can he turn it down?!

ROOSTER:

Trout's a dick!

PEARL:

I didn't know he retired!

ROOSTER:
Right! The poison will make him tired!

(RUTHIE *enters the bicycle shop with the bicycle from the train. The music covers the sound of the bell on the door. Neither* PEARL *nor* ROOSTER *turns around.*)

PEARL:

Then what?!

ROOSTER:

We break into Jack's barn!

PEARL:

What if it's locked?!

ROOSTER:

We'll blow it up!

PEARL:

We'd kill the horses!

ROOSTER:

We blow it up
a little!

PEARL:

You'd kill the horses a little!

TROUT: *(Offstage)*

Toss me that weight!

ACE: *(Offstage)*

I already ate!

TROUT: *(Offstage)*

what?!

ACE: *(Offstage)*

what?!

TROUT: *(Offstage)*

turn down the music!

(The music volume gets lower.)

ROOSTER:

You have a better idea?

(RUTHIE accidentally knocks something over or drops the bicycle.)

PEARL:

…we could ask his wife.

RUTHIE:

wait, are you the woman who—?

ROOSTER:

fuck. How long has she been standing there?

(*In one movement,* ROOSTER *grabs a chair and a bunch of rope and pulls a gun on* RUTHIE, *who spooks.* ROOSTER *points to the chair.*)

ROOSTER:

sit.

(RUTHIE *does.* ROOSTER *hands* PEARL *the rope.*)

ROOSTER:

tie her up.

PEARL:

Me?

ROOSTER:

I'm holding the gun.
You want to hold the gun?

PEARL:

…no. heavens-fuck.

(PEARL *wraps the rope around* RUTHIE, *who squirms.*)

RUTHIE:

let me go
we can pretend this never—

ROOSTER:

yeah, we can't let you go

RUTHIE:

what

ROOSTER:

you know too much

RUTHIE:

I didn't hear anything

ROOSTER:

bullshit

RUTHIE:

I won't tell

ROOSTER:

Ha.

RUTHIE:

I just came to see if you knew whose bicycle this was.

PEARL:

Yeah, that's mine.

RUTHIE:

what happened on the train?

PEARL:

nothing

RUTHIE:

but

PEARL:

I was just looking for some privacy
he's the one who made it—

ROOSTER:

Enough! Don't give her information. She's gonna
go home to her husband and undercut the whole
goddamn plan.

PEARL:

what're you gonna do, kill her?
Maybe she wants to help us.
Do you want to help us?

ROOSTER:

Why wouldn't she be on his side?

PEARL:

I mean, I've met him…

ROOSTER:

Bullshit.
She has everything. She's got lavender flowers planted along a white porch. She's got acres. She's got room. Why would she leave that?

PEARL:

Maybe she doesn't want any of that.
Maybe she wants to be taken seriously.
Maybe she wants to be the one who rides the horse.

ROOSTER:

This isn't pretend. She doesn't get to put on a black hat, call herself an outlaw, and head for the coast.

RUTHIE:

wait
the coast? really?

PEARL:

Is this how it's going to be? You thinking I'm playing pretend?
I'm serious, Rooster. I'm not going back.

ROOSTER:

I ain't talking about you. I'm talking about her.

PEARL:

You know what I did before I left?
I took the lace overlay from the foot of my bed and tied it to the weathervane
because I'm so sick of things that are pretty and can't do shit.
Anyone who sees that won't need to look under the fabric to know a storm is coming and the direction it's coming from.

ROOSTER:

Great. Fucking fantastic.
Then you decide what's next, Hurricane Pearl.

RUTHIE:

If it's about riding the stallions—
Jack would let you try,
if I asked.

ROOSTER:

Ha. He promise you that?

RUTHIE:

yes.

ROOSTER:

He lets you ride those stallions, and I'll eat my boot.

RUTHIE:

Jack's different.
The Jack you met isn't the real Jack.

ROOSTER:

So you've ridden those stallions.

RUTHIE:

no
not yet
but—

(*A loud crash from the "gym". The music cuts out.*)

ACE: (*Offstage*)

I'm fine! I'm fine!

PEARL:

Rooster. They're—

(ROOSTER *starts untying the ropes.*)

ROOSTER:

fuck fuck fuck

(RUTHIE *stands, as* TROUT *enters.*)

TROUT:

we got any ice?
oh—sorry. Customer.

(*Beat*)

RUTHIE:

thank you for your help
with the bicycle.

ROOSTER:

Don't go spreading my secrets—
my / technique around town.

PEARL:

What Rooster means is
if you don't have the wind in your hair soon…
come on back, and we'll get that
chain reattached.

(RUTHIE *takes* PEARL's *bicycle and exits.*)

ROOSTER:

fuck.

TROUT:

what?

PEARL:

(*Muttering to* ROOSTER)
she took my—

ROOSTER:

nothing.

TROUT:

ice?

ROOSTER:

In the freezer.
You know, where it stays frozen in this
fucking desert.

three.
meanwhile, back at the ranch

(COW *eats some grass.*
It tastes terrible.
She constructs an arugula salad with balsamic vinaigrette.
She looks over her shoulder to make sure the other cows
aren't watching her, mocking her.
She takes a bite. It's not satisfying.
She's bored with the same old shit.
She does yoga to feed her spirit.
It kind of makes her feel better
but only for a moment.
Then,
she notices some dandelions on the other side of the fence.
Like a beacon. Like a sign.
Something different. Something more. Something better.
She looks over her shoulder to see if anyone is watching.
She goes over to the edge of the fence.
She reaches for the dandelions. She can't get to them.
She wanders up to the fence and tries to reach for them
again.
She still can't reach.
But she has to have them.
She tries one more time.
Then, she decides to ask JACK.
Maybe he doesn't know that there is a whole world beyond
the fence.
Maybe he doesn't realize that she could be free.
She runs off to find him.)

four.
behind the barn

(*Night. Back behind the barn on* JACK's *property.*)

(JACK *has a shovel. He piles dirt on top of what looks like was a very large hole. Was.*)

(*Shadows across his face. Dirt on his hands.*)

(COW *approaches, delicately.*)

(JACK *hears her footsteps and spooks. He's awfully jumpy.*)

JACK:
You damn near scared me to death.
What are you doing back here?
Shoo. Get out of here.

(COW *hesitates. She is determined to show* JACK *the dandelions on the other side of the fence.*)

JACK:
What? I said get.
There ain't nothing to see here, you hear me?
Nothing to see.
I'm out here in the middle of the night
and everything just turns to dust.
Stop looking at me like that.

(COW *doesn't move. She understands what it feels like to be desperate to control her own life. She understands more than he can imagine.*)

JACK:
I said stop it! Get out of here!
Get!
Don't make me—!

(JACK *approaches* COW *with the shovel. She takes a couple of steps back.*)

JACK:

Oh, now you understand.
Yeah? Is that what it takes?
Get out of here! Get!
Don't come back!

(RUTHIE *enters with* PEARL'S *bicycle, wearing her new black hat, as* JACK *threatens* COW *with the shovel.* COW *runs away.*)

RUTHIE:

Jack?

(JACK *whips around to see* RUTHIE.)

JACK:

that stupid cow
always acting funny
she wouldn't—

RUTHIE:
so you threatened her with a shovel?

JACK:
I'm sorry, thought I was the one in charge of the livestock.

RUTHIE:

sorry
she's never given me any trouble, so I thought—
you're working too hard

JACK:
What are you doing out here anyway?
It's late.
Why aren't you at home?

RUTHIE:
thought you'd want to put the bicycle in the barn.

(JACK *takes the bicycle from* RUTHIE. *He doesn't put it in the barn.*)

JACK:

later.

RUTHIE:

I can do it.

JACK:

Don't go in there. One of the stallions is
sick.

RUTHIE:

sick? what kind of sick?

JACK:

A cold. We can talk about it later. I'm working.

RUTHIE:

It's late.

JACK:

Yes, Ruthie. It is late.
This is what it takes for us to have what we have.

RUTHIE:

sorry

JACK:

Don't come looking for me
when all I'm doing is making sure that we can keep
living our lives

RUTHIE:

sorry
It just
looked like you were done digging so I thought it
would be
a good time

JACK:

Well it's not.
I'm not.
(Beat)

I'm tired is all.
I'm just tired.

(RUTHIE *goes to* JACK.)

                              RUTHIE:
you can talk to me

                              JACK:
I can't

                              RUTHIE:
why not?

                              JACK:
… because.
I'm busy
that's all
go on home
I'll be there in a bit.

(*Beat*)

                              RUTHIE:
Do you like my hat?
Brand new.

                              JACK:
It's nice.

                              RUTHIE:
I'm worried it's a little big
that it might blow off in the wind,
when Cyclone and I carve through the desert.
(*She tosses her hat near* JACK's *feet, as a kind of truce.*)
what do you think?

(JACK *picks up the hat and puts it back on* RUTHIE's *head, sweetly.*)

                              RUTHIE:
Thank you, sir.
not sure how I can possibly repay you.

JACK:

I can think of a way.

RUTHIE:

yeah?

JACK:

mhm

RUTHIE:

but I wouldn't dare
compromise my marriage for any old ranch hand

JACK:

ranch hand, huh?

RUTHIE:

mhm

JACK:

I see
so you're married?

RUTHIE:

I am

JACK:

and you wouldn't consider leaving him for me?
not even after I put that hat on your head with such a
delicate touch?
think of the ways these hands might be useful, darlin'

RUTHIE:

wouldn't dream of it.
but you could let me ride one of those stallions instead
I could ride behind you
wrap my arms around your waist

JACK:

no ma'am I won't

RUTHIE:

You won't?

JACK:

no ma'am

RUTHIE:

come on
we'll slice through the night
I'll race you down the train tracks
We don't ever have to come back

JACK:

what's gotten into you?

RUTHIE:

you said you'd let me ride them
didn't you?

JACK:

when did I say that?

RUTHIE:

didn't you?
didn't you promise?

JACK:

well, you can't.
women ride bicycles

RUTHIE:

I know that.
this is different

JACK:

how you figure?

RUTHIE:

because it's
it's me.

JACK:

that doesn't make a difference

RUTHIE:

it doesn't?

JACK:

no

RUTHIE:

It always did before. Or I thought it did.
That's it?
You're choosing all this over me? Over us?
You know what I've given up for you?
Shame on you.
You've changed.
You've become like every other man in this town
and I'm getting pretty tired of waiting for you to come
back

JACK:

I gotta get back to work.

RUTHIE:

Back to work?! Stand here and listen to me!

JACK:

don't go getting all hysterical.

RUTHIE:

Jack Owens, I expected better of you.

JACK:

here it comes

RUTHIE:

are you smiling?
don't you dare fucking smile.

JACK:

baby doll, if it ain't this, it's the picture in the paper
and if it ain't the picture, it's something else.

RUTHIE:

what are you trying to say?

JACK:

I'm saying get mad so you can forgive me already,
won't you?

RUTHIE:

the stallions are in trouble, you know

JACK:

they're fine
it's a cold, I told you—

RUTHIE:

they're in danger
they
could be stolen

JACK:

Ha. Are you crazy?
Who would dare?

RUTHIE:

I'm not crazy.
This is real.

JACK:

let's pretend
let's pretend this is real
what do you propose we do?

RUTHIE:

we take the stallions somewhere
you and me
we ride them out of town
away from—

JACK:

I see what you're doing here, honey.
you ain't riding these horses.

RUTHIE:

you promised me

JACK:

when? when did I promise?

RUTHIE:

while we were making plans

before you had a penny
you promised me

                        JACK:
so back before any of it was real

                        RUTHIE:
it was always real.

                        JACK:
things change.

                        RUTHIE:
you said, once we were famous
once we were known

                        JACK:
that's the thing, though, isn't it?
we ain't famous. we ain't known.
I am.

(Beat)

                        RUTHIE:
things do change, don't they?

(RUTHIE *leaves* JACK *standing there.*)

five.
outside the fence

(COW *stares out beyond the fence at the dandelions. She has
a packed bag.
A little ways away,* RUTHIE *stands, looking up at the stars.
Trying to decide what to do.
She spots* COW *in the distance.* COW *doesn't see her.*
RUTHIE *takes a couple of steps toward* COW, *but before she
can say anything…
Through a feat of bravery, cunning, and force of will,*
COW *leaps into the world.*

She looks around. She's free.
She's fucking free.
She dreamt about this.
But she never thought she could—
She never thought she would.
Holy shit, it's wonderful. She dances. She skips with cow-glee. Her eyes are wide with cow-excitement.
She grooves.
She sees RUTHIE *staring at her.*
The women share a moment of recognition.
Then, COW *runs off.*
RUTHIE *watches her go.*
She decides.)

six.
in the desert

*(*PEARL *and* ROOSTER *stand with guns in the middle of the desert.)*

*(*PEARL *also has a bag of some kind.)*

*(*ROOSTER *has her hand on a pistol in a holster.)*

(The sun beams down and creates waves on the horizon. Rattlesnakes make noise in the distance.)

ROOSTER:
you think she ain't betrayin' us this very minute?

PEARL:
no, I don't.

ROOSTER:
I do. I think she's runnin' a finger down his jawline saying "you and me, baby".
I got a bad feeling about this.

PEARL:

what's it gonna take for you to trust her?
because I'm starting to take it personally.

(RUTHIE *comes running on.*)

RUTHIE:

I'm sorry
I'm sorry
I'm late, I know.
I'm sorry.

ROOSTER:

Jack know you're here?

RUTHIE:

no.

ROOSTER:

so where does he think you are right now?

RUTHIE:

waited for him to leave

ROOSTER:

what do you know about the coast?

PEARL:

Rooster, she's with us
leave her be/ and let's figure out how to—

ROOSTER:

you don't know she's with us
this might all be some sort of revenge for whatever she
thinks you did with Jack on the train

PEARL:

It wasn't like that

ROOSTER:

I know that
but—

RUTHIE:

it's not revenge.
it's for me.

ROOSTER:

didn't answer my question.
what do you know about the coast?

RUTHIE:

I don't know.
never thought about it.

ROOSTER:

she lacks vision

PEARL:

She's here. That's saying something.
I'm inclined to trust her.

ROOSTER:

why?

PEARL:

because we can't afford to be suspicious of our own,
Rooster.
We can't. We'll be stuck here forever.

(*Beat*)

RUTHIE:

We're not gonna kill him, right?

PEARL:

No. Just poison him a bit. It's not even that much.
Just a teeny tiny little bit of poison.

RUTHIE:

(*Referring to* ROOSTER)
I want to hear her say it.
promise me.

ROOSTER:

…we ain't going to kill him.
I don't care about killing him.

But after she makes a request like that
I ain't handing her a gun.

PEARL:

Rooster. What's she supposed to do?

ROOSTER:

Rattlesnake bait. I don't care.
I hand her a gun and she could shoot us.
You think of that?

PEARL:

She wouldn't do that.
(To RUTHIE*)*
would you?

RUTHIE:

I haven't yet

ROOSTER:

what's that supposed to—

(RUTHIE *reveals a gun of her own. Chaos.* ROOSTER *and*
PEARL *scream as though ready for war.* RUTHIE *panics. She
tosses her gun on the ground as a gesture of peace.* PEARL
and ROOSTER *calm—collect* RUTHIE'*s gun.)*

RUTHIE:

I took one of Jack's
an old one
found it in the attic

PEARL:

she's sharp,
and resourceful
and she's got a great hat

ROOSTER:

alright, alright.
fine.

(ROOSTER *slowly returns the gun to* RUTHIE*.)*

ROOSTER:

shoot rattlesnakes.

RUTHIE:

I've never—

ROOSTER:

you with us or not?

RUTHIE:

I am, but

ROOSTER:

then
shoot rattlesnakes.

(ROOSTER *returns* RUTHIE'*s gun. The women hear a*
rattling. ROOSTER *points to a rattlesnake. She reaches for her*
pistol. But before she can even think about aiming, RUTHIE
has already pulled the trigger. She hits it)

RUTHIE:

Sorry.
loud.

(*Beat.* PEARL *runs over to the dead snake.* ROOSTER *is*
unimpressed.)

PEARL:

heavens-fuck that was a nice shot

ROOSTER:

lucky shot

(*A rattle in the distance.* PEARL *spots the rattlesnake by the*
base of a cactus.)

PEARL:

maybe it's easier than it looks

(PEARL *lifts her rifle. She shoots at the snake. She fires off*
four shots before the lights on the cactus flicker and go out.
PEARL *looks pleased with herself.)*

ROOSTER:

poor cactus never stood a chance

PEARL:

close enough.

ROOSTER:

snake went that way
maybe you could follow it home
become best friends
braid each other's hair/

PEARL:

we'll find another one

RUTHIE:

how many do we need?

ROOSTER:

we?

PEARL:

what's your problem?

ROOSTER:

so she can shoot.
doesn't mean we need her.

PEARL:

means it's easier

ROOSTER:

don't care if it's hard

PEARL:

yeah? then why're you still here?

ROOSTER:

was waiting for my moment
this is my moment

PEARL:

she can help

ROOSTER:

she doesn't owe us nothing
she could change her mind
she ain't even thought about what the coast might
mean
what it might take

RUTHIE:

'course I have

ROOSTER:

what?

RUTHIE:

the horizon
that's what I've thought about.

ROOSTER: *(To* PEARL*)*

you tell her to say that?

PEARL:

no

(They hear a rattle.)

PEARL:

where is it?

ROOSTER:

watch your step, it could—

*(*RUTHIE *spots the rattlesnake come out from behind a rock near* ROOSTER*'s feet.)*

RUTHIE:

Rooster!

(Before ROOSTER *can react,* RUTHIE *shoots the snake.)*

ROOSTER:

you just—

RUTHIE: *(Facetious)*

lucky shot?

(Beat)
Listen, I'm not changing my mind.
I promise.
I know what it's like to make plans
and to wait and wait.
If you don't get to the coast
it won't be because of me.
You can trust me.

(Beat)

ROOSTER:
the horizon?

RUTHIE:
the horizon.

PEARL:
well okay then
storm's comin'.

(ROOSTER collects the snake and brings it over. It's small.)

ROOSTER:
storm's comin' indeed
nice shot

PEARL:
reminds me of Ace
(She holds the snake how one might hold a snake, if one were insinuating that it were a small penis.)
just a little guy...

RUTHIE:
who's Ace?
(To ROOSTER)
your boyfriend?

(PEARL laughs. ROOSTER is not amused.)

ROOSTER:
Let's just fucking test one, okay?

PEARL:

a little rattled?

ROOSTER:

get the milk.

(PEARL *begins to unload the bag. She hands* ROOSTER *a glass jar of milk.*)

RUTHIE:

how much poison is it going to take?

ROOSTER:

not an exact science.

(ROOSTER *chops off the snake's head with vengeance and hands it to* PEARL. PEARL *squeezes the snake into the milk. She winces.*)

PEARL:

ew ew ew
ewwww

ROOSTER:

calm down, it's dead

(*The venom is red. The women hold their breath. The milk turns pink.*)

PEARL:

that's...pink.

ROOSTER:

shit fuck

RUTHIE:

I don't think I can get him to drink that

ROOSTER:

no shit

(RUTHIE's *thinking...*)

PEARL:
we need to dilute it somehow?

ROOSTER:
heat it?

PEARL:
freeze it?

ROOSTER:
mix it with something else?

PEARL:
water?

ROOSTER:
or whiskey?

RUTHIE:
we need a cow to eat it, that's what we need

ROOSTER:
what?

RUTHIE:
sure, I mean—

if you put a bunch of dandelions in a glass of milk, it'll turn it yellow.

PEARL:
but when a cow eats a bunch of dandelions and then you milk the cow

RUTHIE:
the milk is white.

ROOSTER:
that was cute what you did right there finishing each other's sentences and all

PEARL:
rancher's daughter

RUTHIE:
rancher's wife

ROOSTER:

but even if that is true
you know a cow that doesn't belong to your husband?

RUTHIE:

actually…I do.
I mean, she used to belong to Jack, but
now she doesn't.
She ran off.

PEARL:

a free heifer

ROOSTER:

so we're just supposed to entice her with some
delicious poison?

RUTHIE:

No. We'll tell her the plan.

ROOSTER:

and what makes you think that's gonna work?

PEARL:

it worked on me

RUTHIE:

and me

(Beat)

ROOSTER:

well, then
if you were a cow
who just left the ranch
where would you go?

seven.
the saloon

(*A saloon. Filled with men and shadows of men.*)

(*Something thick and honky-tonk on the radio.*)

(COW *enters, hoping to find someplace safe. The outside world is not what she expected.*)

(COW *drinks at the bar, slightly disguised and drinking alone. Men leer at her. She can feel their eyes.*)

(TROUT *and* ACE *outside the saloon.*)

TROUT:

Repeat it back to me

ACE:

I got it I got it

TROUT:

Repeat it back.

ACE:

No trust. Fine. The plan:
We convince him to let us bring your supple horse,
Pomegranate

TROUT:

Peaches

ACE:

right, Peaches
over to meet his stallions,
make us some super ponies, and voila
Jack gets a cut, Rooster—diamond in the rough that she
is—gets her bicycles back, you get a new dream, and
maybe you cut me I don't know let's say fifty percent
of your future profits?

                    TROUT:

thirty

                    ACE:

forty-six

                    TROUT:

thirty

                    ACE:

deal.

                    TROUT:

and I do the talking.

                    ACE:

we'll see

                    TROUT:

Ace—

                    ACE:

my friend, I'll tell you what I tell all the ladies that I
have known—
this semen
will be worth the trouble.

(ACE *and* TROUT *enter the saloon.*)

                    ACE:

Your finest spirits!

                    TROUT:

where is he?
you said he'd be here

                    ACE:

He will be.

                    TROUT:

when?

                    ACE:

eventually

TROUT:

we don't got a meeting, do we?

ACE:

not exactly a meeting in the exact dictionary definition
of a—

TROUT:

Great. Then how do you know he's gonna be here?

ACE:

Instinct.

TROUT:

This was a dumb idea.
Never should have put you in charge of any of the—

(TROUT *watches* ACE *spot* COW. ACE *winks at* COW. *She
turns away, disgusted.*)

TROUT:

exhibit A

ACE:

Hey hey hey
it ain't a formal meeting
but now we get to embrace the element of surprise.
Trust the plot and buck up.
Jack Owens can smell fear like it stepped in manure.

TROUT:

hate that you're calling it a plot

ACE:

the scheme

TROUT:

worse

ACE:

the plan, the path, the journey
our quest.

TROUT:

let's just forget it

ACE:

what do you want from life, Trout?

TROUT:

he ain't here
and we don't know for sure that he's coming
why even bother—

ACE:

You know what I want?
I want an adventure.
A life that doesn't fit on a headstone.
And a woman to bang into a headboard—but that's
besides the point.
What do you want?

TROUT:

Doesn't matter what I want

ACE:

Boo

TROUT:

It doesn't.

ACE:

oh I'm sorry—I didn't realize you were the champion
of fucking mutton busting. My mistake. I thought I was
talking to a fucking cowboy. But apparently, you left
all your "cowboy" at the rodeo, so pardon/ me

TROUT:

I want a new dream, okay?
Without rodeo, all I got is normal.
An ordinary day used to be—
You ever feel your heartbeat in your ears?
That's what my normal was. It was all blood, dirt, grit
and holding my breath
for eight seconds of almost-dying

my fingertips clutching the cliff's edge of life
everything damn near silent
until I got the ground under my back
sky above my face
the crowd bursting through
all screaming my name.
That was normal.
Now I got a bicycle shop I don't wanna run
and a sister who hates me for it?
That's supposed to be my new dream?
That ain't my normal.
My normal's bigger. Special.

ACE:

then trust me and hold your horses for
five, four, three, two—

(JACK *enters the bar.* ACE *goes to straighten* TROUT's *tie.*
TROUT *slaps his hand away. They stand.*)

ACE:

told you

TROUT:

you got lucky

ACE:

luck is a special talent of mine

TROUT:

I'll do the talking

ACE:

Guys like him are my specialty

(TROUT *ignores* ACE *and approaches* JACK.)

TROUT:

sir

JACK:

gentlemen.
(*He downs his drink. Gets another*)

TROUT:

Maybe it's hard to recognize me off the circuit, but—

JACK:

I'm supposed to know who you are?

TROUT:

Yessir, thought you might

JACK:

Let me ask you something… You know who I am?

TROUT:

I do

JACK:

well okay then
anything else?

(TROUT *is speechless.* ACE *jumps in.*)

ACE:

sir, it's a goddamn—
I mean a goshdarn goddamn pleasure to meet you.
You look just like your picture
only less black and white
more pigmented. Don't you think, Trout?
Don't you think he's much more pigmented?

JACK:

I'm very busy, gentlemen—

ACE:

Trout, the man's in a hurry
don't you think he looks much more pigmented?

(*Beat*)

TROUT:

umm definitely. Rosy cheeked.

ACE:

Sir, what you said in the paper was so inspiring
so exciting

so motivating that if you could give us a moment of
your time—
we know you're in a hurry—man like you has to be in
a hurry
got a lot of acres to—

JACK:

your point?

TROUT:

we have a proposition for you

JACK:

that so?

TROUT:

Hear us out

JACK:

Why should I do that? I don't even know your name.

ACE:

Good point. I'm Ace, that's Trout.
We have a question for an important man such as
yourself.
Are you ready for the deal of a lifetime?

JACK:

I'm listening.

ACE:

Picture this, if you will.
Money. Lots and lots of money.
You see that jukebox?

(JACK *turns around to look in the back corner of the saloon.*
His back remains turned toward the door for the next
exchange, so he doesn't see RUTHIE, ROOSTER, *and* PEARL
enter. RUTHIE *spots Jack—They have to think quick.*)

JACK:

Yes, I see it.

ACE:

Now picture that jukebox
but made of gold.

JACK:

Okay…

ACE:

You see that lamp over there?

JACK:

the one hanging from the—?

ACE:

Yes, sir. Now picture that lamp
but made of gold.

TROUT:

Ace, maybe we should—

ACE:

One more one more
That chair.

(All the women turn, to avoid JACK's glance.)

JACK:

I think I get it

ACE:

Made. Of. Gold.

*(The women make their way cautiously toward COW at the
bar. They need to get her out of the saloon without being
seen.)*

JACK:

Do you have a point?

TROUT:

Ace, tell him our—

ACE:

Sir, it's about your reputation

JACK:

what about it?

ACE:

we can help you build a legacy
because let's face it
reputations come and go
right, Trout?
today, you're famous,
tomorrow you might be—

JACK:

I need another drink
(*He gets up to go to the bar.*)

ACE:

Damn, you're so tall. Has anyone ever told you that?

TROUT: (*To* ACE)

What was that supposed to mean?

(PEARL *intercepts* JACK *before he gets to the bar. The women
sneak out over the course of their conversation.*)

PEARL:

Howdy, stranger.

JACK:

place like this ain't suitable for a girl

PEARL:

Good thing I'm not a girl, then.
I'm an outlaw, remember?

JACK:

prettiest outlaw I've ever seen
You know, I still have your bicycle

PEARL:

don't need it

JACK:

I get it

PEARL:

what

JACK:

if I have your bicycle
you always have an excuse to come back

PEARL:

you think I like this

JACK:

you know, those posters with your face on 'em are
getting mighty close to town.
What are you gonna do when someone turns in
daddy's little girl?

PEARL:

threatening me?

(The women have exited. PEARL goes to leave.)

JACK:

what are you running from? hm?

PEARL:

outlaw never tells.

JACK:

you'll always be a girl to me, darlin'

PEARL:

we'll see.

*(PEARL tips her hat to TROUT and ACE on the way out.
JACK returns to the table.)*

JACK:

what were we saying?

TROUT: *(Testing him)*

who's the girl?

JACK:

hm? old friends. You know how it is, gentlemen.
Trains are such sociable establishments these days.

Now, if only the locks on the compartment doors were
as reliable as the company.

(*Locker room talk.* TROUT *goes to say something. He doesn't.*
He laughs. He downs his drink.)

ACE:
sir, back to what we were saying.
we think that it would be in your best interest
if you would allow us to bring over Trout's horse,
Pomegranate—

TROUT:
Peaches

JACK:
for what?

ACE:
pony/love?

TROUT:
breeding.

JACK:
oh, gentlemen.

ACE:
we can pay
in theory
depending on how much it costs.

JACK:
I don't think you realize what those horses are worth.
Unnatural how big they are.

TROUT:
You didn't even hear our
scheme.

JACK:
Can't say I'm interested in schemes.
Haven't got the time for a couple of rodeo clowns.
So if you'll excuse me, I should be getting back to check

on
my stallions.
(He exits the saloon.)

ACE:

It was not lost on me that you called it a scheme just
then—

TROUT:

We have to
do something

ACE:

Trout, let me explain something to you—can I explain
something to you? —
there's this thing called the food chain

TROUT:

We're just going to let him belittle us?

ACE:

What else can we do? You want to go over there, hide
Pomegranate behind a cactus, and borrow his stallion
like it's some kinda library book? Because I don't see—

TROUT:

…yes.

ACE:

wait, really?

TROUT:

We'll go steal—

ACE:

borrow

TROUT:

borrow one of his stallions.
let it
meet

(ACE *makes some sort of gyrating gesture.*)

TROUT:

Peaches.
Then...we put it back.

ACE:

Trout, I don't use this word lightly.
I don't use this word ever.
This is a word I just made up.
Scheme-tastic.

eight.
before the heist

(A tableau—silhouettes.
JACK, at home, out on the porch.
RUTHIE comes up to meet him.
RUTHIE offers the milk to JACK.
JACK drinks the milk. Big, greedy gulps.
It makes him very tired.
He passes out.
RUTHIE checks JACK's pulse.
RUTHIE gives the sign to the women.
PEARL, ROOSTER, RUTHIE, and COW on a mission.
They approach the barn with the same kind of choreographed
swagger that an action-movie star walks away from an
explosion. Let it have music. Let it be movement.)

nine.
meanwhile, back at the ranch
at the barn

(Meanwhile, back at the ranch.)

(TROUT and ACE skulk around the barn.)

ACE:

we gotta hurry.
coyotes come out at night, man.
you wanna mess with that shit? didn't think so.

TROUT:

did you tie up Peaches?

ACE:

I am mostly certain that I might have remembered not
to forget to tie up Pomegranate.

TROUT:

Don't move.

(TROUT *turns back to check on his horse.*)

(*Meanwhile, the women have started to make their way
toward the barn. Quietly, so as to not wake* JACK *from his
poison-stupor.* ACE *spots* COW, *but he thinks it's a coyote.*)

ACE: *(Whispering)*

Coyote...
Trout...?
Trout...? It's a coyote. It's a—

(ACE *raises his gun. He shoots a fearful warning shot in the
air. All of a sudden,* RUTHIE, PEARL, ROOSTER *and* COW
come into view. TROUT *comes running.*)

TROUT:

what the—?!

ACE:

oh my god thank god
it's a cow
it's not a coyote it's a cow

(ROOSTER, TROUT, PEARL, ACE *and* RUTHIE *all speak and
act simultaneously on the following two pages:*)

ROOSTER:	TROUT:	PEARL:
What the fuck you two doing	What are you doing here?	
	What are you—	Y'all need to leave *now*
None of your fucking—		Rooster, they're gonna—
	What the Hell do you think you're	You ain't borrowing anything
I'm not fucking around	what's going on?	
Trout, get out of here		Heavens-fuck
I ain't telling you shit, so just—	*You* get out of here, we have a—	We're not messing around
Don't make me	What the fuck is this about?	Leave!
	What are you goona do?	Now.
(Pulls the gun on TROUT*)*	*(Pulls his gun on* ROOSTER*)*	*(Pulls her gun on* TROUT*)*
	What the Hell did you get that?	Don't you dare
Shoot me, I dare you	Another one?	
	Put it down	
Make me		You put yours down

ACE: RUTHIE:
And the beautiful
Rooster

                         We need to be
                         quiet
We just need   Cow, can you—?
borrow

You even know   Please, we—
what's in that
barn?

Y'all don't even
know what you're
getting in the
middle of

Much as I love
having you
around

Whoa now, why   You two can't be
the aggression?   here

We're not going
anywhere

(Pulls his gun on
PEARL*)*

Watch it—my   we have to be—
aim is never   quiet
truer than when
I shoot for love

What the—?

(RUTHIE *takes out the key, while* ROOSTER *and* PEARL *hold off the men with guns. She slides the giant barn door open. It reveals nothing. An empty space. The horses are gone—turned to dust.*)

RUTHIE:

It's empty.

Am I crazy?

Where are they?

(ROOSTER, TROUT, PEARL, ACE *and* RUTHIE *all speak simultaneously again:*)

ROOSTER:	TROUT:	PEARL:
What the fuck	Where the hell did they—?	How is that possible?
What did you—?		Now what are we doing to—
	Me?! Nothing!	

Every time you show up, I get stripped of everything I got	I didn't do nothin', Rooster	We're not the problem here
Now I ain't got nothing left for you to take	This ain't my fault	
Nothing ever is, is is?!		Just get out of here already

ACE: RUTHIE:
Empty? Empty?

You're the ones
who threw a
wrench in what
was otherwise

A flawless plan   Please, stop
                       yelling

Whoa whoa   I don't know if
whoa

We were just
trying to get—

(*Out of nowhere, a gunshot.* COW *is hit.* JACK *appears out of the shadows. Before anyone can process what's happened,* JACK *captures* RUTHIE *from behind and holds her in front of him like a shield.* ROOSTER *and* PEARL *are torn between* RUTHIE *and* COW, *who's bleeding badly.*)

ACE:

oh fuck oh fuck oh fuck
run, man, run

(*In the chaos,* TROUT *gets hit in the face by* ACE. *They manage to run off.* TROUT *looks back once.* ROOSTER *sends him off with a look in her eye.* PEARL *and* ROOSTER *try to tend to* COW.)

RUTHIE:

run! run!
Please!
Go! Please!

JACK:

you've got ten seconds
or I shoot you both too

PEARL:

let her go

JACK:

ten

RUTHIE:

please / make sure Cow is safe

JACK:

nine

PEARL:

he's going to kill her

JACK:

eight, seven

ROOSTER:

he won't

he can't
>   JACK:

six
>   PEARL:

Rooster!
>   JACK:

five, four
>   RUTHIE:

take cow! she needs help!
>   JACK:

three
>   ROOSTER:

let's go
>   JACK:

two
>   RUTHIE:

go!
please!
>   PEARL:

but—
>   ROOSTER:

you heard her.

(PEARL *and* ROOSTER *run off, holding up* COW. JACK
throws RUTHIE *to the ground.*)

>   JACK:
You want to tell me what the Hell is going on,
what the Hell you were doing with Pearl Hart and
those rodeo clowns?!

>   RUTHIE:

nothing

JACK:

Nothing? Nothing.
Funny, sure as Hell didn't look like nothing to me.

(JACK *grabs* RUTHIE *and brings her over to the train tracks and begins to tie* RUTHIE *to the train tracks.*)

RUTHIE:

let me go.
Jack. Jack. Please.

JACK:

Trying to steal the goddamn horses
after I trusted you

RUTHIE:

Trusted me?!
You've been lying to me this whole time.
The barn is empty.
I'm going to tell. I am. I'm going to tell everyone that
Jack Owens isn't anyone.
I'm going to tell everyone to forget your name.

JACK:

And who's going to believe you? Hm?
That's assuming you get off these tracks before the
10:14 comes on through—

(*A train whistle in the distance.*)

JACK:

Right on schedule.

RUTHIE:

you wouldn't
you can't
Jack, seriously
Jack
please
what are you doing?

JACK:

What does it look like I'm doing?
I'm upholding the law.

RUTHIE:

you're not going to leave me here
you're not
I didn't do anything/
there aren't any horses to steal!

JACK:

you didn't do anything?
how can you say that?
you think I wanted it to go this way?
you think I like this?
you think I imagined having to tie my wife to the
tracks?
you did this.
I can't have you ruining my reputation.
Worked too hard for it.

RUTHIE:

where are they? what did you do to them?
what did you do?

JACK:

I didn't do anything!
They died.
Okay?!
Turned to dust, so I buried 'em.
They must've been sick or something.
Wasn't natural how big they were.
It wasn't my fault.
It wasn't my fault.

RUTHIE:

they died?

JACK:

knew you'd be sorry

(RUTHIE *draws her gun, her arms inhibited a bit by the ropes.*)

JACK:

Ha. You even know how that works?
You gonna shoot me? Go ahead.

(RUTHIE *can't get herself to do it. She doesn't lower her gun, though.*)

RUTHIE:

I'm not sorry.

(*A train whistle sounds in the distance.* JACK *begins to walk off.*)

JACK:

Well, I am.

(RUTHIE *yells after* JACK. *He doesn't turn around.*)

RUTHIE:

I'm not sorry! I take it back!
I take back every word every breath every syllable my
tongue my lips my teeth my gums my throat my air
my sound my space my throat my throat my throat
and my fingers and my hands and my nails and my
body every inch of my skin I take it back I take back
the room I'm not sorry I'm not sorry my teeth aren't
sorry my canines the sharpest parts of my body the
pocketknife the hidden tools the tools the tricks and
the times I pretended I take it back I take back the
knives and the file and the scissors and the hidden
tools the hidden tools and the things I knew how to do
and pretended I didn't I take it back I know how I do
I am the hidden tools I'm the pocketknife I'm drawing
blades I'm drawing blood all the blood all the blood I
apologized for having for leaving behind for trailing
behind me down me in me I'm not sorry I take it back
I'm not hidden I won't hide I know I know I can I

am these knots these knots you tied these knots and
I'm the knife I'm the blade I told you I couldn't you
thought I couldn't I apologized when I could when
I could better sharper all my tools hidden but not
anymore

(RUTHIE *holds the pistol pointed at the knot. She knows that
if she misses, she's dead. By bullet or by train. She shoots.
It hits the knot. The ropes fall off her. She tosses them aside
and leaps off the tracks just in time. The sound of a train
shooting past.*)

RUTHIE:

Ha. Sorry.
(*She runs off.*)

ten.
the desert

(*In the desert,* PEARL *and* ROOSTER *tend to* COW.)

PEARL:

We should've shot him!
Why didn't we shoot him?

ROOSTER:

Ruthie's the only one with that kind of aim

PEARL:

you could've tried

ROOSTER:

we promised we wouldn't kill him

PEARL:

that's not what she meant

ROOSTER:

we don't know what she meant

PEARL:

what if she's dead?

(COW *moos weakly.*)

PEARL:

you're okay
you're okay

ROOSTER:

she ain't dead
she's smart—she told us to go.
I trust her.

PEARL:

we should've shot him

ROOSTER:

and what if I'd hit her?
then what?

PEARL:

but there was a chance

ROOSTER:

we couldn't risk it

PEARL:

well now he's got her
and we don't know if she's dead or alive

ROOSTER:

she ain't dead

PEARL:

you keep saying that
you don't know

ROOSTER:

I'm sorry that real change has real consequences, Pearl
next time we stir up trouble, I'll make sure everyone
plays nice
and nothing bad or scary happens, so that you don't

have to deal with anything real ever.
that what you want?

(*Beat.* COW *moos again.*)

PEARL:

shh, I got you.

(ROOSTER *kneels down with* PEARL *to comfort* COW.)

ROOSTER:

I didn't mean that.

PEARL:

everything was supposed to be different

ROOSTER:

what do you want me to say?
I wish I shot him
but I didn't.
I'm sorry.

PEARL:

I know
I'm sorry

(COW *moos weakly.*)

PEARL:

so what are we going to—?

ROOSTER:

you stay here.
I'll go back

PEARL:

you can't go alone

ROOSTER:

someone has to stay with Cow

PEARL:

then you stay
I'll go

ROOSTER:

I'm the better shot

PEARL:

but I know him
maybe he'll—

(RUTHIE *comes running up.* COW *sees her first. She moos, points.*)

PEARL:

heavens-fuck
thank goodness

ROOSTER:

you all right?

RUTHIE:

he tied me up.
he had me tied to the railroad tracks.
and a train—

PEARL:

how did you—?

RUTHIE:

I shot the knot.
I shot it clear off.

(*They gather around* COW. *She's dying.* COW *moos. "The horses?"*)

RUTHIE:

the horses are dead.
I think maybe since they arrived.
Or not long after.
turned to dust.

PEARL:

she's lost a lot of blood

ROOSTER:

maybe we can go and—

(COW *moos again. "You have to get out."*)

RUTHIE:

it's okay
we'll be okay
we'll be okay

(COW *looks up at the stars to thank someone or something
for the beautiful ways in which things can change. She isn't
afraid.* COW *smiles. She curls up.* COW *sleeps.* COW *returns
to dust. They cover her with a jacket. They place a dandelion
at her feet. They huddle together around her, saying goodbye.
They take a few steps away.*)

RUTHIE:

what are we gonna do?

ROOSTER:

need to regroup. need to take a breath.

PEARL:

I have an idea.

eleven.
outside the saloon

(TROUT *and* ACE, *outside the saloon.*)

(ACE *munches on a stalk of celery, as he holds some ice up to*
TROUT's *face.*)

ACE:

good thing marvelous Rooster carries most of the
beauty in your family
because your beauty is going to be on hiatus for a
while

TROUT:

and whose fucking fault is that?

ACE:

someone's in a mood. And I know our lives were just
in peril—you like that? —but peril is no excuse for
being snippy.

TROUT:

aren't you
angry?

ACE:

of course I am—look at your face—I'm gonna have to
give myself a black eye so I look as tough as you. Give
me a good story for it. Like we were riding through
the desert and a pack of coyotes started nipping at
Pomegranate's ankles when—

(TROUT *pushes* ACE's *hand away from his face.*)

TROUT:

forget it.

(ACE *puts the ice back on* TROUT's *face.* TROUT *hits him
harder, this time.*)

ACE:

Hey! What the fuck is your problem?

(ACE *throws a stalk of celery at* TROUT. TROUT *picks it up.*)

TROUT:

seriously?

(TROUT *goes to stab* ACE *with the celery.* ACE *blocks his
blow with another stalk.*)

ACE:

what the fuck

(*The boys sword-fight with celery, until* TROUT *knocks*
ACE's *celery out of his hand.* ACE *rushes at* TROUT *and
tackles him. They wrestle.* "Ow" "Stop it" "Get off me,"
until they release, exhausted.)

(They take a breath on their backs. TROUT *gets up. He offers his hand to* ACE, *who takes it and stands.* TROUT *motions for* ACE *to turn around. He does.* TROUT *wipes the dust off of* ACE's *back.* TROUT *turns around.* ACE *begins wiping the dust off of his back, then his motion slows.)*

(ACE *hugs* TROUT *from behind. A beat.)*

(TROUT *turns around.* TROUT *picks up a stalk of celery at* ACE's *feet. Blows on it to clear it of dust. Hands it to* ACE. ACE *takes a big bite out of it.* TROUT *smiles and shakes his head.)*

TROUT:
The whole scheme was a failure. It's like I'm fucking cursed.

ACE:
man, listen—
I got everything I wanted out of this little shenanigan of ours.
I got to watch the vein on Jack's head pulse like a rattlesnake trying to swallow a fucking horse.
I got a fucking phenomenal story of my endless bravery and cunning to win over your pistol of a sister.
And I got to go on an adventure with my best friend.
I got everything I wanted.
We're not fucking cursed. Those stallions weren't ours. The ranch wasn't ours. That dream was a dream. Single dream. Just one.
You were a champion. That's over now.
We ain't so special, Trout. We gotta try something else or we turn into tumbleweeds.

TROUT:
So we're worthless. Great.

ACE:
now, just because we ain't special
doesn't mean we're worthless.

we're just us.
Trout and Ace.
Two. Guys.
Being Guys.

(ACE *helps* TROUT *up.*)

                    TROUT:
I'm used to feeling like a champion
now, look at me

                    ACE:
you're the most impatient little cowpoke I ever did see.
it's been two days.
you weren't a champion your first two days in the
rodeo,
you were a walking bruise.

                    TROUT:

but I had something
something to work at
now what've I got?

                    ACE:

you tell me
what've you got?

                    TROUT:

I don't know

(ACE *threatens* TROUT *with some celery, good-natured)*

                    TROUT:
okay okay
I got my fame, sorta.

                    ACE:
sixteen-time, I repeat sixteen-time winner of—

                    TROUT:
And I got Rooster, I guess.
Though, she did point a gun at my head earlier—

ACE:

she didn't shoot you.
and if she wanted to, she would've

TROUT:

true.
And I got the bicycle shop, which—

(TROUT *looks up at* ACE, *who is happy for his best friend.*)

ACE:

you got a lot, man

TROUT:

guess, I do

ACE:

now you just gotta decide what you're gonna do about
it.
Get on home. Rest up.

(TROUT *goes to leave. He calls back to* ACE.)

TROUT:

Ace—
There's something else.
I got you.

ACE:

Forever.
I've already got a few bright and shiny ideas for
tomorrow. I mean, it might require a teeny tiny bit of
highway robbery to build up a reputation, but I think
that—

TROUT:

I love you.

ACE:

Love you too.
See you tomorrow.

twelve.
the movies

(*The women sit at the movies.*)

(*The lights are dim, but the movie hasn't started yet.*)

(*They each hold a bucket of popcorn.*)

(*None of them eats.*)

PEARL:

this was a good idea.

ROOSTER:

it was your idea.

PEARL:

the movies are a good place to be—

ROOSTER:

hopeless? desperate?

PEARL:

at least we'll be safe in a dark room.

RUTHIE:

for two hours…

PEARL:

clear our heads.

RUTHIE:

what are we gonna do?
pretend like it never happened?
I can't go back.
Jack thinks I'm dead.

(CALF *comes scooching in in front of them.*)

CALF:

excuse me,
pardon me

PEARL:

Is that…?

ROOSTER:

What the—?

(*The women all stare at* CALF, *disbelieving*)

RUTHIE:

Wait, that's—
Calf?

CALF:

Ruthie
hi

RUTHIE:

what are you doing here?

CALF:

my mom said that if she didn't come home
to go through a hole in the fence.
and so now I'm at the movies.

RUTHIE:

Did she tell you what it would mean?
If she didn't come home?

CALF:

yeah

RUTHIE:

we're so sorry

CALF:

because she died?

PEARL:

yes

CALF:

I know.
It's really sad.
But it's also happy, right?

That's what she told me.
That it would be sad and happy.

ROOSTER:
no one else is curious how the cow is talking?

CALF:
my mom taught me.
she couldn't talk.
she just said "moo".
moms want their daughters to know more than they
did.
so I know how to talk.
Why are you at the movies?
Are you also sad?

ROOSTER:
damn straight we're sad

PEARL:
we need a new life

RUTHIE:
a new dream

CALF:
What was your old dream?

PEARL:
it's a little complicated

CALF:
I'm a talking cow.

ROOSTER:
we were trying to get to the coast
you heard of it?

CALF:
mhm
I'm gonna go someday.
That's what my mom said.

RUTHIE:
Well, your mom was helping us.

CALF:
so why do you need a new dream?
That's a good dream.
You should do that one.

PEARL:
well, it didn't exactly go according to plan

ROOSTER:
your mom teach you any swear words?

PEARL:
Rooster.

RUTHIE:
Point is, we need to move forward.

CALF:
so same dream, different plan.

ROOSTER:
we are fresh out of fucking plans, at the moment

PEARL:
Rooster.

CALF:
It's okay.
I know that one.
moo.
it means
"fuck" and "fuck yeah"
depends on how you say it.
kind of like today.
sad and happy.

ROOSTER:
well, "moo".

(The lights dim. The previews are starting.)

RUTHIE:

she's not wrong.

PEARL:

shh.

RUTHIE:

no, listen.

same dream, different plan.

ROOSTER:

like I said
fresh out of fucking—sorry—"mooo"-ing plans.

RUTHIE:

except we're not.

PEARL:

Ruthie, the stallions are—
D.E.A.D.

CALF:

a lot of things are dead today.

ROOSTER:

of course she can fucking spell.

PEARL:

we've got no way out.

RUTHIE:

but we never had a way out.
we just thought the stallions were our best bet.

ROOSTER:

they were.
until they D.I.E.D—died.

RUTHIE:

but who said the stallions were ever going to be the
way out?

ROOSTER:

every goddamn newspaper and—?

RUTHIE:

the men.
Jack, the papers.
the men told us

PEARL:

so?

RUTHIE:

they're also the ones telling us we can't
that we can't leave
that we'll never make it on bicycle
that the coast is a myth
that we're crazy
that we made it up

ROOSTER:

that we're too fucking emotional
that we're too fucking weak

PEARL:

that we're delicate
that we've got such a pretty figure
why tarnish
why ruin

RUTHIE:

why rush
why leave
why try

ROOSTER:

why complain
hem and haw

PEARL:

raise our hemlines
lower our necklines

RUTHIE:

cover up
conceal

ROOSTER:

dress up
dress down
look down
look away

PEARL:

shrink and wilt
and flower and bloom
all the florals and the lace

RUTHIE:

and the laces and the corsets
and the buttons and the beads
and the eyes of all the needles

ROOSTER:

sittin' on pins and needles
waiting and waiting and waiting

PEARL:

and waiting

RUTHIE:

and waiting
for things to change
being told that they'll never change
that there is no change
that change has happened

ROOSTER:

that we've come so far
that there's nowhere else to go
that this is as far west as there is

PEARL:

that this is it
and it should be enough
and we should be happy
and we should be satisfied

with our bicycles and our place and our things
and the way things are

RUTHIE:

but we aren't.
They are the ones who said that we'll never make it on
bicycle
to that place that doesn't exist
those
liars.
so…

PEARL:

so

ROOSTER:

so that's how we'll go

RUTHIE:

that's how we'll go

PEARL:

two wheels to the coast

RUTHIE:

Are we doing this?

ROOSTER:

moo.

CALF:

you have to say it like
mooo
that's the good one.

RUTHIE:

moooo

PEARL:

mooo

ROOSTER:

moooo

RUTHIE/PEARL/ROOSTER/
CALF:

moooooo! mooooooo!
mooooooooooooooo!
moooo!
mooooooooo!

(After they "moo" for a while. They take a deep breath. They're exhausted. They laugh. Another deep breath. They look at each other. They know what they have to do.)

thirteen.
meanwhile, back at the ranch
at the barn

(PEARL makes her way up to JACK's barn.)

(She finds JACK, drunk, with his back to the train tracks.)

(He can't get himself to look.)

JACK:

what do you want?

PEARL:

you been crying?

JACK:

leave me alone
I want to be alone
I am alone

PEARL:

why do you think that is?

JACK:

it's the law
I had to tie her up
I had to

PEARL:

you didn't

JACK:

Look at the tracks.
Look at the tracks and tell me what you see.

(PEARL *looks over at the tracks. She decides to torture* JACK.)

PEARL:

what did you do?
there's blood
everywhere

JACK:

oh God oh God oh God

PEARL:

you're a monster

JACK:

shut up! shut up.

PEARL:

don't touch me.

(JACK *breaks down.*)

JACK:

it's too late it's too late it's too late

PEARL:

you're a mess

JACK:

good, good
say it again
say it slower say it with your hands on my throat

(*Beat.* PEARL *gets her bicycle from inside the barn. Wheels it out.* JACK *stares at his hands.*)

JACK:

do they look different to you?

you've seen 'em
you saw 'em before
they the same now?
or they look scorched?

PEARL:

what?

JACK:

think the devil's claimed 'em
think I'll be a pile of charcoal before dawn
that's why I'm drinking
burns faster

(PEARL *is disgusted.* JACK *senses it. He can see it on her*
face.)

JACK:

why did you come back here?

PEARL:

for my bicycle
so that you know I'm never coming back

JACK:

I never showed her—
I found a part of a mountain that reminded me of her
and I forgot to tell her
and then I forgot again
and then it didn't seem important.
But it was. It was important.
And I only remembered a minute ago.
And it wasn't my fault. I had to. I had to. It's the law.
What if they found out and I—
But I didn't—
I should—
Oh please please anybody
will you hold me, please?

PEARL:

no
no I won't

(JACK *buries his face in his hands. He gets very small. He's likely crying. He coughs as though he might throw up.*)

PEARL:

Look. Look over at the tracks.
Face what you've done.

JACK:

no, no I can't I can't please
please don't make me please

PEARL:

So that's what kind of man you are.

(JACK *slowly turns toward the tracks. There's nothing there.*)

JACK:

what?
how?
where is she?

PEARL:

You will never see her again.
Never.
Don't let your pain end.
You thought you were a villain?
You're a coward.

(PEARL *goes to leave, wheeling her bicycle alongside her.*)

JACK:

where are you going?
where are you taking her?

PEARL:

Doesn't matter.

She's happy
without you.

JACK:

you'll never
you'll never get anywhere—
not riding on those.

(PEARL *smiles.*)

JACK:

what?

PEARL:

the way you said that.
you believe it so
completely

fourteen.
the bicycle shop

(ROOSTER *collects the supplies she needs.*)

(TROUT *enters.*)

TROUT:

I got something to say.

(ROOSTER *ignores* TROUT. *She packs tools.*)

TROUT:

what's the wrench for?

ROOSTER:

shop's gonna go to shit faster than I thought
if you don't know how to use a wrench.

TROUT:

middle of the night—what's broken what's loose?

ROOSTER:

everything, Trout. everything's broken—everything's

loose.
do none of you see that? do you not see that?
because I'm having a hard time believing that you can't
see what this is all about.
I know you better than that. Or I thought I did.
(She finishes packing and heads for the door.)

TROUT:

you're leaving?

ROOSTER:

'course I'm leaving—

TROUT:

I didn't ask for this

ROOSTER:

sure as Hell didn't do nothing about it, neither

(ROOSTER goes to leave. TROUT stands in front of the door.)

ROOSTER:

I ain't afraid to move you

TROUT:

I never wanted it this way
for you to lose everything

ROOSTER:

I swear

I'll kick your ass harder than any bucking bronco ever
did, if you don't—

TROUT:

I'm your brother. And I never once left without saying
goodbye.
So
if you'd just quiet your big, stupid head long enough
for me to—

ROOSTER:

my big, stupid head?

TROUT:

I'm trying to apologize.

ROOSTER:

well, you're shit at it.

(*Beat*)

TROUT:

I'm gonna be sticking around
trying to make this place into something

ROOSTER:

good for you

TROUT:

Things will be different
if you stay.
I think you could run things out here,
and I can handle all the—

ROOSTER:

Trout—

TROUT:

hear me out

ROOSTER:

no, you hear me out.
All this—this peacemaking
you trying to be here
for me
it's too late.
I don't need it.

(*Beat*)

TROUT:

I ain't special, Rooster. Learned that tonight.

ROOSTER:

for the first time?

TROUT:

yes, for the first time

ROOSTER:

funny thing
when your whole life,
people, men
tell you that you ain't special—you can't do this, you
can't do that
bicycles instead of horses
a funny thing happens
you start to think that maybe you are
that maybe you're a thing they don't know what to do
with
a thing they're afraid of.
I've been told I ain't special for long enough.

(*Beat*)

TROUT:

I'm just supposed to let you leave?

ROOSTER:

Let me? I don't need your permission.
But I'd take a goodbye.
You could understand. That would be enough.

TROUT:

there's nothing I can say to get you to stay?

(ROOSTER *shakes her head.*)

TROUT:

you pointed a gun at me earlier, remember?

ROOSTER:

you pointed one at me

TROUT:

but you drew yours first

ROOSTER:

I didn't shoot it, did I?

(*Beat*)

TROUT:

Write me? Postcards? Something
so that I know you're—

ROOSTER:

Like the ones you sent?

TROUT:

fewer spelling mistakes.

(ROOSTER *nods. She goes to leave but isn't sure how to say goodbye.*)

TROUT:

You think there's ever gonna be a time again when me
and you
live in the same place for more than a couple of days?

ROOSTER:

Maybe. But I don't know how long it'll be until then.
You're gonna be fine.
Don't be a stranger.

TROUT:

Well, you know where to find me.

(ROOSTER *and* TROUT *hug goodbye. She leaves.*)

fifteen.
the desert

(RUTHIE *and* CALF *wait on the edge of town, in the middle of the desert.*)

(*Cacti like a constellation around them.*)

CALF:

what's it like?

RUTHIE:

what?

CALF:

the coast

RUTHIE:

well, no one's ever been
so we don't know

CALF:

then how do you know it's good?

RUTHIE:

that's a
good question.
There are stories about it.
Made-up. Dreams about what it might be like.

CALF:

like what?

RUTHIE:

umm let's see
well, an ocean.
More water than the biggest puddles
more than we could drink in our whole lives.
And it moves.
In waves. It comes out out out
and then back in in in
and it never stops. It moves forever because the moon
pulls it with an invisible lasso.
There's sand—but not like here —
it's purple with flecks of dark grey and silver,
and when it's wet, it tugs at the bottoms of your feet
like it wants to play a game. It's the opposite of a
cactus, of a tumbleweed.
And there's a smell. The best smell. It smells like
like like a warm morning that's been sprinkled with
salt
and put in an enamel pot with a pool of

warm water
like it's been wrapped in a handkerchief that
was sitting on a rock in the sun
like it's been pulled from the earth
and the earth's tears healed the wound.
It's lovely.
And there are fish.
And birds.
And swimming turtles.
And...

(PEARL *and* ROOSTER *have arrived with their bicycles.*
Ready to leave.)

CALF:

And what else?

RUTHIE:

And us.
Soon.

ROOSTER:

thought you said you never thought about it.

RUTHIE: (*To* PEARL)

nice bicycle

PEARL:

couldn't leave it behind

RUTHIE:

we ready?

ROOSTER:

damn straight.

PEARL:

meohmymeohmy.

(*Dawn. The sun is just beginning to warm the dust. The*
cacti yawn and soak it up.)

(RUTHIE, PEARL, ROOSTER, *and* CALF *straddle their bicycles at the edge of town.*)

(*They stand at the edge. Staring out into the vastness of the desert. They take each other's hands. The women work up the courage to step beyond the border, unsure if they'll be struck down by some electric fence or higher being, should they do so. They take a deep breath. They squeeze each other's hands.*)

(*They mount their bicycles, braced for the worst.*)

(*They wonder if it will ever stop feeling like a risk to take a step forward.*)

(*Then, they leave.*)

(*The escape, the journey*)

(*It starts almost as a kind of spin class.* PEARL, ROOSTER, RUTHIE, *and* CALF *on a bunch of bicycles pedaling together to the beat of the music. It's choreographed. The women can hoot and holler. Adrenaline. They're in the saddle, and they're out of the saddle. This is all in unison. And it should look like the most badass female army of bikers you've ever seen in your goddamn life. They're terrifying. They're awesome. They're on a mission.*)

(*Time passes. The dream propels them forward. Until…*)

sixteen.

(*The sound of the ocean. The smell of the ocean. The feel of the ocean.*)

(*All of the colors should change. Music. Temperature*)

(*They've made it. They've made it to the coast.*)

(PEARL, ROOSTER, RUTHIE, *and* CALF *see the ocean in front of them for the first time.*)

(*They've all stopped dead in their tracks.*)

ROOSTER:

holy/fuck

PEARL:

meohmymeoh—

CALF:

moo.

RUTHIE:

wow.

(*They stare ahead. They're feeling every emotion. Disbelief, excitement, grief, monumental joy.*)

(*They land on that last one.*)

(*It hits them all at once. They scream. They jump. They hug. They hug so much, so hard.*)

(*It's everything they hoped it would be.*)

PEARL:

Can you believe it?

ROOSTER:

I can believe it.
I can fucking believe it.

CALF:

it's so big

PEARL:

I almost don't want to touch it.

ROOSTER:

I do. I wanna swallow it whole.
Look at that horizon.

PEARL:

It's everything
everything you said it would be
everything we imagined
Isn't it?
Ruthie?

RUTHIE:

It is.
And something else.
Ours.

(They absorb this. RUTHIE takes off her hat. They take a few steps toward the ocean. The sun rises behind them, in the east, and creates a silhouette. The four of them and their bicycles. They look out at the horizon, as the ocean touches their toes for the first time. They all exhale together, and alone, in this moment of—finally—feeling free.)

END OF PLAY